Maze

Poems

Maze Poems

David Harrison Horton

ARTEIDOLIA
PRESSPRESSPRESSPRESSPRESS

New York

Thanks to the editors
at Catchwater, M58, New Note Poetry,
Otoliths, and Thi Wurd.
for publishing parts of this project

— and to Graeme Nichols
for photographing the maze poems.

ARTEIDOLIA PRESS
P.O. Box 157
New York, N.Y. 10276

arteidolia.com/arteidolia-press

First Edition
Library of Congress Control Number: 2022910036
ISBN: 978-1-7369983-5-9

The maze poem as a form began with letters that I sent to friends in the early 2000s. In 2018, I bought a big blue sketchbook at a small shop and began to explore the form more systematically. Presented here is a selection drawn from that notebook.

The mazes are a form of automatic writing. They are composed in a single sitting: first the maze is drawn, then the text is written to fit the shape. As such, each represents the shape of a single train of thought. The resulting pieces are part poetry, part essay, and part visual art.

They are also intended to slow readers down as they process the words on the page. It's a different way for a reader and the author to interact. I hope you will appreciate this purposeful manipulation of your routine pace, and think about how we connect with words and information, and how our approach to this inputs to their meaning.

To read a maze, start with the letter that is in bold and work your way through the maze. If we look at the first maze in this book, we start with the bold T, then work out "True fact" and following, so we get:

True fact the second person on the moon was a woman but I can't remember her name at the moment only that I heard it from a better than terrible reliable source like where I get all my info these days in the hustle and bustle of a slow suburban daydream.

dhh
Beijing, 2022

a better tha

morf tid

hat I hear

tyl not n

the mome

T True

remember. inact I tubn

amanren

second

terrible reliable source

person on the

bnamowasawnoo m

Maerdyadn

slow suburban

a felts subdan

an the hustle a

is y a d
e se
n to
in f
y m l
t a i
e g
r e I
e h
e w
k i l
r c e

he divorce before t

ter ofeb straeh

ep o w s a n d s k y y

cr r r a b l e e h s c

im y t h i n g w r a

ps r e v e d a s f pe

on e a u t y o g e

sr b e n t n i r l l

ed H u n g o v e o

it s e n i l t u o r

na a g a i n s t t

ms d n a n o o m e h

    t h o u g h t s o f c

m r e c c o s e h t n o e

ally great highwa y

ehwyreveotmetsys

orizon to give a sense of

Left margin (top to bottom): e a n d n o w c o w s o n t h e h
Second left column: s i n g d o w n t h i s r e
Third left column: i u r c n a v i n i m m o

Right margin (top to bottom): e c n a t s i d n a e l a c s
Second right column: h e e w s b r o k e n a x i l o l i c s

pannuymnileveroteris

pinessaspellb

n reckon beyond a deep de

ac Itahtnosaerdoogon r

ying like a heavy satchel fo

yrracmaItah

rtsurfymdnaflesym

ing beyond

A h a n htynahtiw

l a a s d to connect

l t e n yrt I s a n a

m i v d r y, and hum

y o e e I gna, gnik

v n b t a

i s e s m utterly lac

t e e

a t n

h t

efore I set myself right an

n i subsi h th ti w no teg d

ess of looking life frontwise

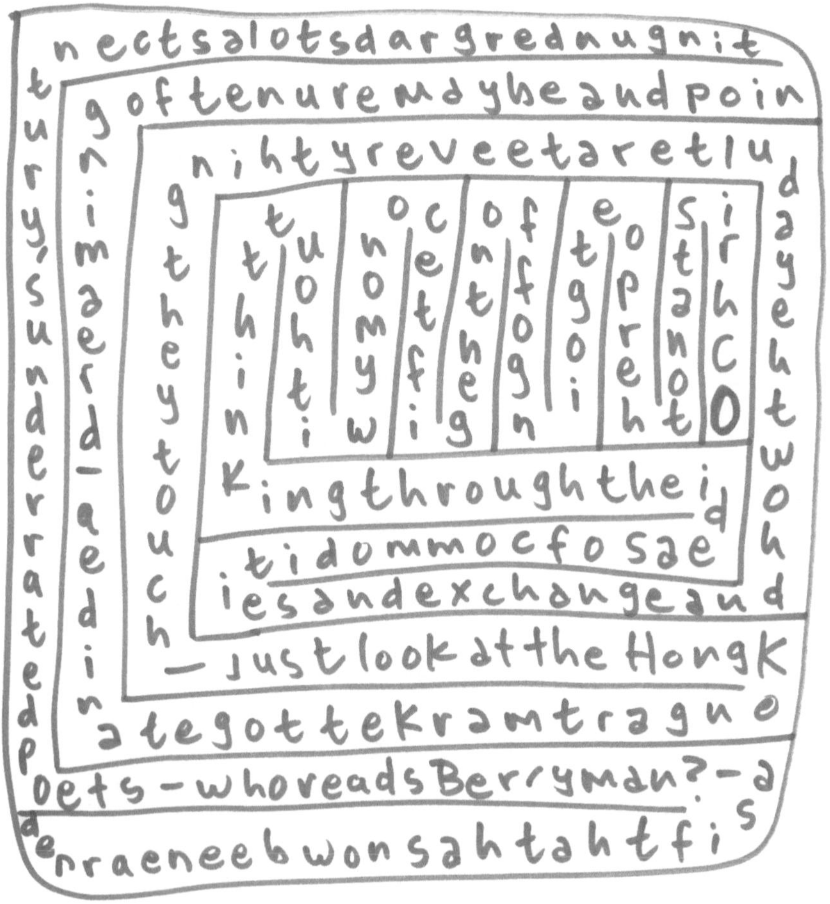

[Spiral / concentric text piece — read in rings]

Top horizontal lines (outer → inner):

nectsalotsdargrednugnit

g of tenure maybe and poin

nihtyreveetaretlu

Inner vertical columns (read top to bottom):

they touch ·· think it ·· touhti w ·· nomywig ·· onetfig ·· conthen g ·· of thegin ·· etgoi ·· eopreh ·· sirhC O ·· dir

Bottom horizontal lines (inner → outer):

king through thei

tidommocfosae

iesandexchangeand

— just look at the Hong K

ategottekramtragn o

oets — who reads Berryman? — a

derraeneebwonsahtahtfi s

Left vertical (outer, top → bottom):

turrys, sunderrated p o d e

Left vertical (inner):

nimaerd-aedin

Right vertical (outer):

d a y e h t w o h · and

cnipe
abish
daeldn
lthisa
lanipr
hatunde
tsedoc

countri
reht
sorino
trop

countries
right
rosino
sport

istening a d y c a r ehsilbu
iebdluo y y i n e f o s dtingP
reallysh J m G d o i tegdni
Inehwsd o t r i s n uldn'tm
owatbir b e e s a a owItah
dniweh t s G e l h ownott
ingoutt d f r a c i nmehts
ratsfomu i f e d r g atdoe
i o e a n e h htdoog
t t g n

Horace are dust so fat lot of
dn aremiehneppOekilsyu
Every few months I sta g
motwohtuobaknihtottr g
e r s s h a m i e n s n
a u s e a t t g v m o i i
s s c n w t h t u e c d r
u d h h t a n e
a a e

knowge | e
uoyg
eadin
rymtn
ppleme
usoty
centl
erdnu
ingar | o
klawf
aloto
gniod
been
ev'I

e t i n t o t h e r e a l w

oday.
tssenis
realbu
emostu
oingabo
gelpoe
esandp
noecin
ngsand
idliub
sugly
esuoh
thtea
iwreht
ahamandIsaac
rbAgnivaelgn
rldsortoftni

ytilae r
w h thisr
e guorh
m ndert
a owaek
d andta
e tnemo
t them
o rofer
g theya
e ereh w

A

l this wn
b ev 'I eli
e een looking
r fsgnihtta
O M one angle tn r

h o n t e
h g u o r
o n e l e n s
n e n w s
t h a t w
e r l y j

a wenotsu
y to focus
g nihtemosno
a mong many
t niyllauqereht o
eresting ways t
g nihtemasehtod o
in a different way

srehtomorfdet a

d ecisionssepar

dnasthguohtes

e chanismtohou

mtnereffidnis p

ro

perhaps

cordah

canworie

elits oh

vers of th

eldnasygel

ve like pul

msgeldna s

ng your arm

ihctawni

your owns k

m i t e m o s

n g e s y o u a r e

a r t s a

e r i n y o u r

v o h n w o r

s e s o m e t i m

r a t s a s

n g e r i n

S re u im

d e s u u o y t a h w o d s
t o d o t h
r d n a e r e n
r e c o g n i z e
y t a h t e
o u n a v e n
c t i o n t o a
c e n n o c o
i o n t o a
h t f o y n
i s a n d i t
t s u J s ,
a b a d b o r i n
o f m r o f g
o f c i n e m a

g n i t a f o i k
n i k o o l s e
l a r p l a c e c
u g e r e h t i l
a r o u n d a l
P M o t s n e h
w t o w e l l t
o n k u o y t
a r i n t o a c i
r t w o l s a e

y o u t a k

Each decision you have ever made has defined the person you are at this moment but the next decision you make frees you from that and offers you a chance at reinvention within each and every turn, there are parameters but no limits, just an accurate measure

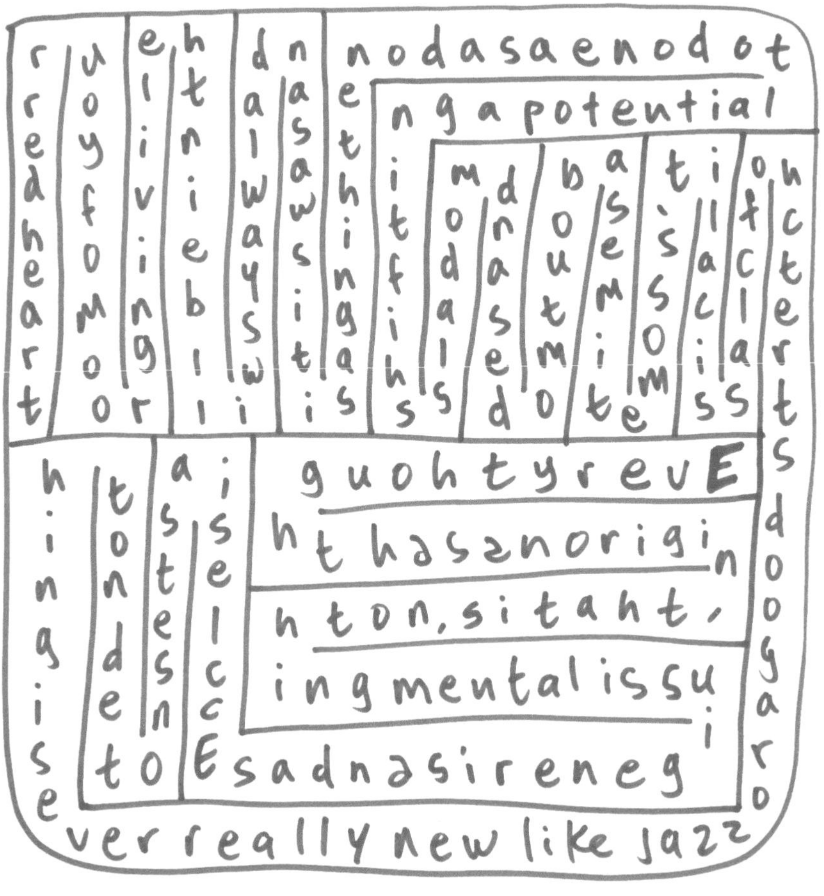

(Hand-drawn spiral word puzzle. Text runs in a rectangular spiral; many lines are written in reverse. Best-effort reading of the letters as they appear:)

Top edge (reversed): **nodasaenod ot**
n g a p o t e n t i a l

Left-side vertical strips (top → bottom):
- r | r e d h e a r t
- u o y f o M o o r
- e l i v i n g
- h t n i e b l i l o r
- d a l w a y s w
- n a s a w s i t i s
- e t h i n g a s

Inner vertical strips:
- i t f i h s
- m o d a l s
- d n a s e d
- b o u t m o
- a s e m i t e
- t i s s o M e
- l f a c i a s s
- o n c t e r t s

Center block (nested lines, some reversed):

g u o h t y r e v E → *Every thoug-*
h t   h a s   a n   o r i g i (n) → *-ht has an origi(n)*
n t o n ,   s i t a h t , → *, that is, not n-*
i n g   m e n t a l   i s s u (i) → *-ing mental issu-*
E s a d n a s i r e n e g → *generations and sad E-*

Lower-left vertical strips:
- h i n g a i s e
- t o n d e t o
- a s t e s n
- i s e l c c E

Right-side vertical strip (top → bottom):
- o n c t e r t s d o o g a r o

Bottom edge (L → R): **-ver really new like jazz**

aps a soul, I mean y

noitonehtotn .i
yasyoubuy i
lgnidrocca
discomfort
rotrofmoc
eretooffer i
htllaedomr ng
onyou've eve

uid idea, something aki
youtobetruetoa
roffleseurto
thatthereisn
nifuoyneh W
mhcumasifiesta

evefolluftracgnip

h r e p , l a u d i v i d n i n a , y t

of a separate entit
isulfero d y r

sd. iffferent thac
ght ?. iorafasth
girenoymnha
efilebdrah
iuosnamun

into a shop p
ndthn

viction
nocfo
dicum
omah
twit
saei
n··r·t

A

e c i t o a h c e h t g n i c
e l e m e n t s a s o p p o r t
t i n i f e d r o f s e i t i n u
i o n o f c h a r a c t e r l i k
v a c r o t u o c s y o b a e
e m a n l i g h t i n g h i s
n e h w e k i l e r i f t s r i f

sti pukcajotyawati gni

Kultur storehouses tuck

somerehw, emimev a

ch like improv dau
um, mroftrade t
underapprecia
nasalrubta
AttimesIloo

e loveforitisint

value and thus th | rehtorosmuseum | st of th | aucoerth | wdri

ae remanyn | et onsiit | tlikeI; | ohwdoisren | niodeh gaudpo sylbis ome love ntomor f

enoyreverfo

e appreciation levelf

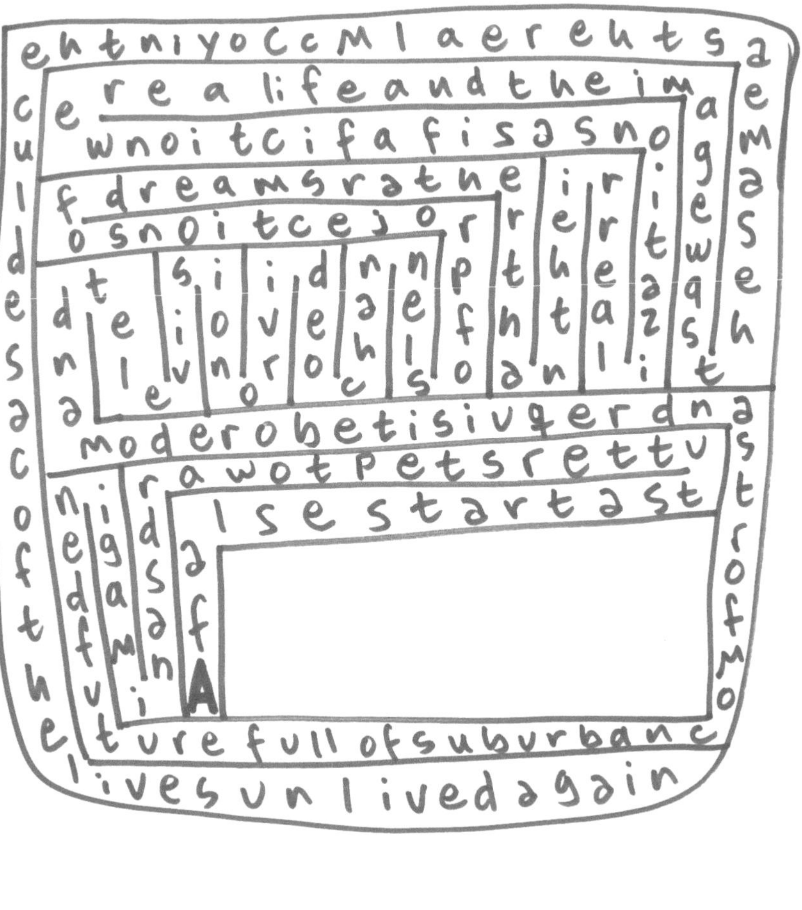

ehtniyoccMlaerehtsa
erealifeandtheim
wnoitcifafisasno
fdreamsrathe
osnoitcejor
culdesacofthe
aeMaseh
agewast
oitazi
rreal
ieht
rthn
rpfo
nnels
dnahc
ideo
ivor
sion
sivo
tele
dena
moderobetisivgerdna
rawotpetsrettu
lsestartast
astrofMo
nedfv
igami
rdsan
afA
turefullofsuburbanc
livesunlivedagain

Withoutti
mugraent,em
entgoes,the
niebonsier
gthattheya
ocretnier

nrobgni
ytheirbe
btcartnoc
fthesocial
odnetrohs
utdrewthe
bdlrowehtn
hereelsei
wynaebreh
swouldrat
ecifforos
efactorie
ntnisklof
ndfiddleas

o n n e c t e d l o
n e v e d e k c o
n a n d y e t t i
n e o m s i e M a
e t i z e d a n d
v i g g n i e b a n d
e n t h e s e c o n

ake up in the ay em.

w m al f m il f y a d y r

i t s e r e t n i n a m o r   r
n   e
g   colors I borrow f   v
p   c   e
a   n i en im t on h t   u   f
l   h   o
e   t   this I paint a y   o
t   i   row g i b y r e v E   M
t   w   d I learned for   o
e   M   l a k a e r b t r a e h   d
       a   be it with a g i   e
       a e t a h t i w r o i   r r

to cover over the b o

he lessoneknows c
tlaususadlroweh t
atallisinfact n
ntgnilangise c

m e   e o   t h   d   i   c n a   n o t t r i g   n i t h   a n s e a g o o   g n i h t d o o
o s   w   r f   h e f i n e   r e   r d i   a s t

g nidnuosnerisadnaet a   a n
e h   en't even left t   t h
r t   v ahdnasage ✓   e h
e n   **A**ll lit up like   h b i
w e   ehwyadanoesuo
ere squirrelssetto h

tdrahoseraesohtaed

All I eve r
wanted
a s a working
ue oliphant bu

there aren't any.

anoitidnocomirpo

s you know
d forget a
dniftuo
ingarepa

to come by and

(surrounding letters: nt ig in q; y ou h a v e; i y n a e; o t e n o c e g; an t o r v e s t; a e r o t; a n a v e r a) egnarehtno

r s l and no indL

s f e K c o

o r l

n o M

, m

s t the da

t h ehw s4

h o n a nick e

o u omsawl

u g htsamoun

re p a d n a y e n

corpdi
(T)ry
gni
toe
nsn
are
ent
sha
oep
fatn

ess, aCamero

o n o s i b d n a e g a r

Me li huwth guo r

osotdet   in the ga

Methingserious

ob
oss'tahtnamye
idebecausen
Issgnihttel
ntosomething
htyehtne
blerwh
ənenəsi
Everyone
secontinuetocu
əhbərcruoyt
ndfromuourveryh
outəndpleə
bənoer'yoyti
omegoodshi
noerəyo
inky
tsirwəəMUh

. w o n o s t o n t u b d l o t n e

m a n k n   o d   e o n c e o f t

u h r   n o   l a t a l l e t

t y f o   w n d   s s a g e s t o

i c a p   l a d   a p r e g n o l

h e c a   e d n e s   r r h y m e i n

t g n   d a i   e v o e c n a n

a r d i   g e   r e f o r a s s o

g   **A** v e c t o r a n d a v o r

e   t s n i a g a t e s x e t

r   a s e r i e s o f m e d

s   i

n o i s u l c n o c l a v e

playacti
e renttuo
upidity
tstahtll
hatwith8
wytsanth
sdownrig
tesfisem
ansometi

ntw io ej nt up gn li lom ns oit tut itsnoc.

while it ever y

ces it on eno

ue st an irbt

hemselves to

hcjmsayas o

ing s
me kn r in
Ist hi a it
oo thi c a
fre si k g
nd Th k e
etrofema
hwnoisivaes

Journal. entri wrapped u

wh s if d l s.o

rriday.so Fstine

o ensure a blue sky

u i n e g a e m r o T l e M s i e r u

of self-imposed struct

secnerrucer eht nidet

ters trapped or libera

e gat ive as it r

naylirassece

dthat's not n

nasyadesent

k and die one of

B er a ekil wonk uoy

need of progression or po

retaehtroamenicsitni

both is a story in | roztlamhcsfodli | sortheposterchi | caraphctteke | kcisPu | take | enoge | your | deton | Sronce | redtdy | uMsA | reallyhashaltot | htiwodott | Perspective

A

senilrevelcwefatsae

o landachoiceroleorat l

e of everythingelsepus

S i r e n

n o s s e l s c

e f a m m e a i l e f h o w t e
b a s e h m a i t s e f t h d y u t
o c y o n e c i l i n t a o n o e
t e r n b a m m s e o t n a u r
s d e e w h p e y h s a s s
d t v i m l n e e e e o
e h e t t i e o i i c n
e a i r r r v i i a
n d n o o i e v l
t f g w r d n a
v u s w n s s
n l o i
t t s f t
o e g
r v n
e d i o i
r e t n r t
a v i a e
h e h r e
a r t b
o r e i n
r w d
b a f o g n i n t a e b n d

dnanees lla, segnahcentni

swith&hope for continuity

i e r e h T
S m o r e s
d n a w o n
m o r e o n
a , y a w e h t

ings like futur

a gnitnalpe

nd eventua

, stsevrah l

family mea

yardnas

ers of tha

a t times 2

fo ecruos
surety or
isuoc stie
, which wi
ws2odll
e contemp

llamsruotnuocewask

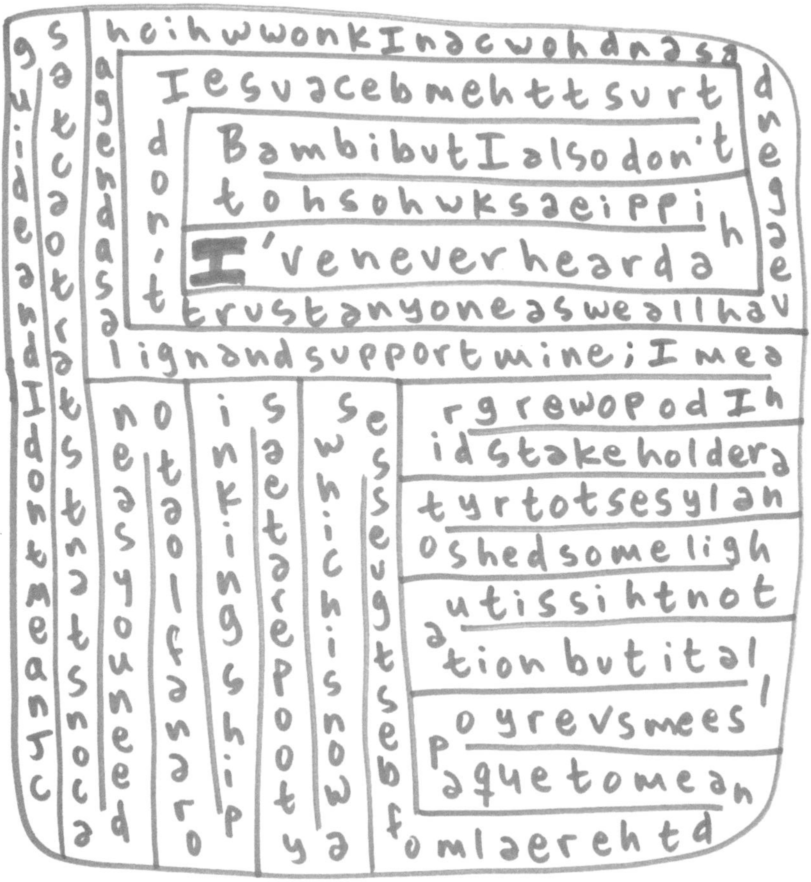
hcihwwonkInacwohdnasa
Iesvacebmehttsurt
Bambibut I also don't
tohsohwksaeippi
h
I'veneverhearda
trustanyoneasweallhav
lignandsupportmine;Imea
rgrewopodIh
idstakeholdera
tyrtotsesylan
oshedsomeligh
utissihtnot
tionbutital
oyrevsmees
aquetomean
omlaerehtd
guideandIdontmeanJc
satcaotratstnatsnoca
agendasa
don't
dnegaev
neasyouneed
otaolfanaro
inkingship
saetarepooty
swhichisnowa
esseugtsebf

oy fi mekomsyenruo j .

s l i a r t y p p a h

u g o t e m k i n d o f

. j II w w t s o p a n o n w o

snanufollufleh c

r you with a sat

of el oh ti bb are

hen it down th

w e r e d q u e s ... t i o n s

or a reaso n

f g n i k o o   o

u s t a r t l   o r w o

o y e c n ⬤

r u p a t e y e s r

tions and second h

v o n t t e k c e B d n a

e l s t o w e i g h y o u d

ect ri ad ev cei er to er n fi on us b a t
t i v e o n w a r d c h r i s
e r i d i o s n a i t s
e r s o r t h e l a s t
o n s i L e h t e M . i t
s M a d e t h e f i n a l . T
a r s r a d i o a n d T
e t i b b b a r g

g h s o m e
g u o r
e s t h
m o c
s a g e
s e m e
t t h
u b y
u l t
a f s
a l i
n g i
e s
h T

g n . i h c t a w f o s y a

a g n i k o o l r o V

o comfort or move me

tnikagnihtynag

e outer preventin

htforaefeht, yt

Exiled   o a   er
         int ni ti ior

n tsisisats

e root of th

ent, yrrow

wind that r

botsesuf

tions, a breeze movin

estnemniatretne, ech

en from a closed window

(left vertical columns, top→bottom): y S S t e m s o f r e l a

(second left column): d l o d n a s d r a

(inner lower-left columns): pedcupob · marcotn · shairi · frniwol

(right inner column, top→bottom): n t t w h e n d w o n s e h t g

(right outer column, top→bottom): o d r i f t a l i t t l e d a

...not mapped out with assumptions and foregone conclusions but something that requires love.

...a little more genuine... but rather so... her parents so different from... denote... the light... right... Michael... straw hat... shirt... resemblance... in the pictures of her friend... doing the right... answer to this moment... which is a human condition among man...

There should be more works dedicated to the men and women who drive snowploughs like how China had a female tractor driver on the one yuan note for the longest time - all the money has Mao's face now, but that's a different discussion - tractors snowploughs the work we need and never celebrate any More I mean Carl Sandburg died a long time ago and the snow needs ploughing and there should be joy

way, but not of winter or sec 14

ing as the human
htonotesolcsar
king of nothing o
nihttaeh s'nus e
nocean under th
anihgiheenkgn
ing or just wadi
ruselpoephti w
re are beaches
ehtdlrowehtn
somewhere i

nois
'ofle
elfa
sstr
isee
inas
roda
char
iawd
ting
arof
retu
fonr
bloss
smo
ndact
yfivi

t i t n a w u o

e m a y b e y

k i l , t e e f o

i t s o w n t w

n o k i a w o t

e a d y, a b l e

you know wh

t i w o d o t t a

h yourself i

e m o m e l d i n

n t s, you have somethin

n o k r o w o t n a l p a f o g

a s t t h e n · e l t a e s u a · g e r b e c a · n o l e l i h w · l i t t l e w · a t s u j e u n · t o c o n t i

t s s l e f · o r e . i t f · f e b s d n · o j e c t e · r p a s e m i · S o m e t i

```
c lonely, like it was c
    t d n a s n i a r  T          h   i   n   t
    r a i n s t a t i o n s       i   n   g   o
    l n o y l e n o l e r a       n   y   t   g   B
       if you've ever s          e   r   o   n   e
    emitemostnep                  s   t   g   a   i
    in or on one, te              e   s   e   y   j
    c, ylenolelbir  r             N   a   t   n   i
                                  e   w   b   e   n
d n a t | l o serewstekciteh      w   I   a   h   g
ing   | s | doutso I waited an    y   a   c   S
cit   | r | uoh 15atog yllan if d e   n   k   M   b
ket back to my baby's arms        a   a   f   o   u
                                  r   r   r   r   t
```

ecitnawsdike

creamandt

uJstludae

stwantana

revnoctlud

sationandt

rasnoiLeh

sandafewbirds

fehtllifots

yaddnevesS

robhgieneht o

, securityblanket

unilekilyawan

hisacomforti

ihwdetcepxee h

thisalladdstot

e b l o w i n g a

Bur
dnadael a
r l I v e s i s
and gninnis
dsomehow this

rameast h
barsgode
rkatnoth
dnagnioth
thesquiri
acssleri
amperofft

wd si saelitufsierutsegl
a that no
eh wlevo o ateventhissmal
ht onn te htediceauoyerof
it x i D oob outofthehouseb
hi K get rtahtgnihtemos
ts o se A slow coffee f
so ge em éfacysubani o
bt et o add a dimension
vn b l
iasa es purpose to the
o wa er atsaeltaroya d
uy ys carry around as i
k kruledidooga f
nu ed around every cor
n
sness httu a nistidnabekilre
b F a
ere's coffee and it's warm

On a day like this one, Saginaw is everywhere you are not, a sum of negative definitions and potentialities to help you gain bearings of just where you might be and whether that is a question that interests you very much as you look out the window to another grey sky and make plans for another day in this non-Saginaw

r o o c n i g n | gnahehttuo
i m n t t t h i | entworking
e e s a h f a g | momtahtni e
s m t h e l t h | lways ther e
a e i t d s g t | aerauoyes
s t t s u e r e | iddlebecau
y u t l e v v | mehtnitr
o v e r o f

ou desperate | ♥oucan'tsea

ekamotyrtyl
chaoslookpre
lredroroytt
y with systems a
o esnesadn
f aestheticsy

nt sa ik M
rebeveluo trainedtop atce omfort lrekrama eashackle ooradra

Printed in the USA
CPSIA information can be obtained
at www.ICGtesting.com
LVHW080754011023
759528LV00020B/170